Rosalie Was All Night

Without the Light

Volume I

1965 to 1987

Rosalie Was All Night Without the Light

Volume I

1965 to 1987

Arthur R. Marinello

Copyright @2015 by Arthur R. Marinello

Published by Rivershore Books

ISBN: 978-0692390528

This book was printed in the United States of America.

INTRODUCTION

I began to think, just recently, of continuing in some manner (or is persisting a better word for it?) to write my version of a poem to the end that I would, sooner or later have a collection of poems. Other more specific goals began to enter the picture. One of them was to use this form of writing to serve various functions: to express feelings, of course, but also to be biographical, historical, and to provide commentary.

I should think it obvious that for one reason or another I write in a certain way, even if there is some development of sorts over the years. Obviously, I eschew, without totally avoiding, rhyming and symbolism and various other techniques frequently associated with poetry. I like flowers as much as most people, but poetry is another matter for me. I simply want to tell a story which can be readily understood. For me, poetry has, or can have, a lyrical spirituality to it which is admirably, blessedly, suited to an honest representation of the feelings and experiences in the life of a human being.

A.R.M.
January 30, 1988

A scene in upstate New York, 1996.

PREFACE

It is quite surprising to me to be publishing this volume with writings which go back fifty years. What were conversations with myself and were never intended to be shared with others. But, here we are. And it's just as well.

A.R.M.
January 18, 2015

TABLE OF CONTENTS

ON PSYCHOTHERAPY

Wednesday
January 13, 1965

I often wonder how this work is done.
Do I prod and jerk or sit and wait.
Can I be honest and open about it all,
Or is it true, as has often been said,
A patient must not know.

TO BE A KID THESE DAYS

Thursday
January 14, 1965

I wonder what it's like to be a kid these days
To have adults do so much for you
Like negotiating a crosswalk with a sign held high.
            (the oncoming traffic is tremendous,
                        of course.)
Why, when I was a kid there was none of this.
I was free as a bird and I knew it.
My morning walk to school was my walk –
            nobody else's.
I was alone responsible for handling any
eventuality
            (there were hardly any autos).

That's not all. It seems to me, in retrospect,
            that the youngsters of my day had a
            wholly different view of adults.
There weren't the paragons of virtue or
            stability in our eyes that they're
                        made out to be today.
Each adult seemed to have his foibles
            (he was human)
Some were totally irrational and we could see it.

What happens to a kid if he doesn't know this.
If he thinks he needs to depend so much on adults
If he doesn't know what they're like.
They're not any better, so far as I can tell –
Than were the adults of yesteryear.

They're just segregated today – sectioned off –
They live in separate areas – totally different
locales.
Some of these adults never even see children
themselves –
       which, of course, doesn't help them either.

But aside   from all this –
What happens when a youngster feels
      that the adults in the world
      are dependable – whether or not they are.
Does he think of himself as strong –
      or does he see others as the
      source of his security.
If so, does this make him any the weaker –
      is he fragile?

ON THE S.C. CAMPUS

Thursday evening
January 14, 1965

A few moments on the old campus – not many
                            really
Just enough for memories to start – coming in-
    one follows the other.
There was that rainy day – so unusual in California
The Daily Trojan reporter interviewing students -
    to find out their reactions.

Then the tree-lined area – at the rear of the gym
That seemed the same – in a sea of changes.

Many memories – just a few moments
Enough to realize – really – that I hadn't come
                    to know the place.
I had more or less just passed a bit of time there –
Enough though – to feel it.

THE CHANGE

January 7, 1969

It's very definite the switch to mod.
The definiteness is meant to convey sharpness
                    and clarity.
One would think the switch to these new ways
Is clear on one point.
They know what they're doing.
They know what they want.
They make no bones about it.
They'll take the consequences.

Consequences - ?
Really there are no consequences.
The thing – is beautiful – rational – clear.
Unfettered by the stinking chains of the past
With all so pure and simple –
So honest.
Consequences, really, won't occur.

They can't.

LEFT BEHIND

January 8, 1969

She couldn't wait.
Life was too short.
There were things to do.
Things to buy.

He was so restrictive.
He couldn't get her the things she wanted.
He was violent, suspicious.
He held her in.

And taking care of the rest of them –
Someone else could do it.
She couldn't stand it any longer.
She was gone.

Without her they flourished.
Demands that stifled were no longer felt.
There was life.
In the end – a pot of gold.

A VITAL THING

January 9, 1969

It's not the tribulations that I mind –
The upsets
The repeated arguments, the blow-ups.
Misunderstandings come and go,
And differences of opinions can rightfully exist.

No two people are meant to be identical –
          one with the other.
How much more so when there are more than two
And possibilities for conflict and misunderstanding
          are increased.

Yes, misunderstandings – once, twice – three –
          a hundred times.
Unresolved?   Fine!
That happens.
Never resolved: Then something must be lacking –
Something vital.

THE LEADER

January 13, 1969

I search, like many others, for an honest man.
I search, unknowing.
I have need of an honest man.

Inside me is a picture of a truly honest man.
He is courageous – he is skilled too –
        he is knowing – he is efficient
            he is warm, human.
He sees a problem clearly.
Given the opportunity, he can rally a people
            to a cause
                intelligently, wisely.

Oh, what good fortune when it happens.
We cannot go on this way –
But, give us this leader.
We can tell when he comes.
I'm sure I can tell.

THE SACRIFICE

January 17, 1969

I bemoan my circumstance
Yet I am whole.
I dread tomorrow
And sacrifice today.

I could have starved a thousand times
But never have.
I could have laughed a thousand yesterdays
I muddled through.

There is a fear of the unknown
Which needs not be.
This waste of time –
This ravaging of courage and of strength
Is witless.

It is to fail a promise.
It is beneath the dignity
Of the hope of man.

PANIC

January 31, 1969

She cannot wait.
The terrors are too great.
There is a panic there that no one can subside in her
Unless you can.
But will you now?
What? Wait, you say?
But then she's off.
There must be someone who can faster do
      what she has left undone.

The signs were there.
The signals could be read.
What was she doing then?
Why so deaf – so blind?
What was she buying with her precious time,
That now, full circle, comes and wants
      its payment now?
And, she, unused to paying mind to her
      despairing self
Seeks someone else to do that chore.

THE INWARD LOOK

February 17, 1969

This is the inward look.
I see you have it.
You do not look outward.
Do you hear?

You cannot go on this way, you know.
A little more and you will be
Isolated totally.
Is this your goal?

Oh, this is not your goal –
Well, then, let me say
I quite agree – from certain signs I see
And, pleased I am as well.

You will look outward now?
You'll try to meet
What heretofore to you has been
An overwhelming mass of misery?

You have a question as expected.
How is this change to be effected?
Pray, why not tell me how.
You see, you've just begun to do it now.

THE SEARCH

November 7, 1969

My brain is dull
When I seek to find
Goals for my existence
In this world around me.

Nor can my vision penetrate
The clouds around myself
So that I can tell
The sort of person that I am.

If I get specific
Things get clearer.
When requirements are recognized
There comes a certain solidity.

Anchors of this sort
Are indispensable.
To search beyond them may be to meet
With unresolvabilities.

ST. GENEVIEVE'S

January 16, 1970

I would like to tell the priests at St. Genevieve's
The new priests, that is
The ones who've come since the building of the
                              new church.

That while this new church is large
And might give one the feeling of a degree of
                    awesomeness, or grandeur,
                              or even, distance,
From the people, that is.
It really shouldn't.

The people who built this church
Or, one might say, whose pastor so decided
Are the same who regularly went to Mass in the
                              old church.

If you went into the old church and could visualize
                    what it once was like
It would become apparent that this old, this
                              former church,
Would have been more communal in nature.
The people closer – to each other – as well as
                    to their priests.

In point of fact, it was a less formal relationship
                    all around.
The priests, now that I think of it,
Did seem to feel closer to their people at the time.
If memory serves – not a one of them left the
priesthood
                    in those days.

As the new church was being built
Some parishioners were impressed
At different stages – pleased.
There was grumbling also,
About the cost
About its large scale
About failure to have a voice
About future needs.

But one day it was completed.
Soon it was dedicated.
It was blessed with
Pomp and circumstance.
The Cardinal himself came.

Also, it served for a Gregorian Convention.
A powerful new Mass was sung.
By three choirs, too;
With a fine director – composer,
But this was when we were barely out of the old
church.

It took some time to realize
Perhaps a year or two
That, on occasion, a priest –
Perhaps a new one – because we've had
        so many new ones
Might just be –
Struck by the bigness there –
Here in this new church of ours –
And as he might stand there –
              losing –
                      missing –
That glue that – common to us all –
                    binds us –
That so might we.

THE RELUCTANT BUREAUCRAT

February 6, 1970

I'm not here because this is the kind of job I like.
I'm here because they put me here.
Somehow – someone has to do this work.
I'll listen to your case now.
Be specific.

You say you'd like your application
                      to be approved.
You feel your request is proper
Oh - - - - - - urgent, rather.
You were misinformed by the operator
                      when you called
And only realize now - - to come in person
Past the due date – to see what could be done.

I must tell you the rule is hard and fast.
No exceptions are allowed.
If you had just returned from war
It might be different.
Or, if the government required – we'd consider it.
But, in your case
You're just too late.
I have no choice.

A PROPER STATUS

February 20, 1970

I had a gift
I let it lie - fallow.
I neither cared
Nor gave it thought.

Sometimes, this gift I knew was there
Seemed to rest upon a parallel -
Next to me.
Yet, something like a stranger -
                    it to me   -   or I to it.

At times, I grasped it –
                    used it,
                        let it go –
        like a plaything - -   of small significance.

What are its qualities - unsuspected
That inveigh against rejection?
Does it have feelings, stomach, soul   -
That demand nourishment and love -
A proper status for its role?

DARE WE THINK

February 24, 1970

Dare we think of one another
In this tortured maze of life? –
Really see the place of someone
Other than ourselves?

Dare we more than mouth the phrases
On the brotherhood of man,
For to go beyond is, least of all,
Uncharted land?

Dare we spend much time at all
Very far from our own interests
Lest we fall into oblivion
To consider someone else's?

The best that we can manage
Is to fashion from our bag of tricks
Some bit or piece which in our innocence
We deem benefactory to him we serve.

Accepting without serious question
That what we offer him we serve
May be to our profit, more than his,
And may do harm to all.

U.S.C. "THOUGHT PAPER" Dr. Pullias

January 13, 1972

I've read an awful lot of books
And taken courses too
The knowledge and opinions gleaned
Should help the quest for truth.

The books, these days
Are most impressed
By the rightness of their cause
And, many, too are nobly put
In terms of wisdom and critique.

But which to buy
In terms of thought
When Illich says "remove the schools"
While Montessori calls for structure?

And what to make of Walden II?
Has Skinner gone berserk?
Are we to live as happy slaves
To operant conditioning?

But hold a bit.
There's Summerhill:
A freedom tract come out of Neill,
Whose background was too strict.

But, then we make another turn
With Leonard's talk of bliss in school,
Majestically combining
The freedom of the Scotsman
With the slavery of the rat.

It seems I'll have to learn the truth
Some other way.
I'll have to do a bit of thinking,
And maybe go to class.
But, best of all, live three lives,
As Man goes slowly past.

THE PRINT

1975-76

I feel that I have been on some ancestral clock
Not pre-ordained or culminating
A cultural or genetic past.
But something else.

There is a sense of schedule,
Which up till now has been
Neither obvious nor obtrusive,
But masked by other things.

There is an urge to reach a point
Demanded by a force,
Which up till now has seemed to be
The press of circumstance.

A matter of the human realm,
Of age or stage in life,
To meet or fail to meet,
The pace of ticking of one's time.

A man must make his mark in life,
Or get this done by now,
Or leave to those who follow,
A place from which to grow.

There ought to be security
By such and such a time
A point at which one has achieved
The goals of modern man.

If this be true for most
It does not hold for all.
I seek not a blissful rest
A pause for balm or peace.

The calm sojourn or frantic tour
Are alien to my thoughts.
The quest for youth, eternal youth,
The thirst for power - - - - foreign all.

This constant inner strife
Undiscernible till now
A strange attempt to match a print
With line uncertain to the view.

TO MY FAMILY ON CHRISTMAS DAY

1977

This is the one hundred and ninetieth Christmas,
That, together, we share
The sum of all our Christmases
The center of our communion
The symbol of our hope, our love, our caring.

There are fifty-seven Christmases for me,
The first seven of which preceded
All the others,
When I could not have imagined
In my journeys through Manhattan's parks
And Jersey's fields,
That soon was to be born someone
Who would first parallel
And, then, share these holy days.

Those were the times when Christmas was
                         wintry with snow
And full of Santa Claus
And Christmas stockings;
When coins and coal were given
And though surely they were humble gifts
Were fully Christmas and joyful then;
Christmas being, as ever, in the spirit.

There was a Christmas forty-nine years ago
When two of us,
My elder brother having wakened me,
Went to see if Santa had yet arrived,
Or, as was hinted, might not really come.

We found the stockings empty
And returned to bed.
The discovery made.
Santa was parental.
And all such matters, had, thereafter,
A sense of the familiar.
Yet, somehow, in that greater familiarity
Were still mingled,
Joy, anticipation, mystery and love,
A fascination with the magic of giving.

The first Christmas I spent with your mother, kids,
Took place thirty-one years ago.
It was a lovely time.
The air was filled with the excitement of
          romance and reunion.
Your mother cut class for the only time,
To meet a train which, cross-country,
          had borne me home, from California.
Surely, romance was in the air.
Brooklyn style.

On Christmas, we saw some friends - -
Fred Forner probably - - -
Maybe Joe Giunta too.
And then we came to the home of
          one of mother's aunts,
                    Aunt Laura,
Wherein lived, I think, her grandmother,
          then in her early eighties,
Who, later, a half year or so later,
          was at our wedding,
Who, on that Christmas Eve,
          had her family concerned,
                    that wed, again, she might,
A suitor having pressed his suit.

CHRISTMAS 1979

Mom,
I ask you - - - - is this the greatest Christmas ever?
Maybe not in one way - - because the greatest
                                        was the first.
Is this the greatest Christmas ever - - - - -
                                        for you?
Or was it your first - - - - or some other?
Or great as one was - - - - - it could be forgotten
          if you're like me   - - and I think
                    you forget things too.

But how about if each Christmas is
          the cumulative total of
                    today's Christmas
          and all Christmases past?
That's not bad.

Dad

TO JACKIE'S CLASS

1981

Here it was - - - my birthday - - - and I had
                all these things
        presents and birthday wishes -
From people I knew - - and - - people
            I'd never seen before.

Especially some people in this fourth grade class
Way out in Newhall.
I really didn't know them –
            tho I knew their teacher - - -
            since she was born.

Anyway, I decided I should write them a poem
                    to thank them.
I used to write a poem every once in a while -
And - - - I thought it would be easy.
Really, I thought it would.

But, as you can see - - - - it isn't.
The last time I wrote a poem was - - so long ago - -
            I got out of practice.

So, I'll just say this to your class.
Thanks for the birthday presents and wishes,
And, also, if you're a poet,
        you'd better stay in practice,

                signed,
                    the father of
                    you-know-who.

Jackie 1996 in California.

ALMOST SIXTY TWO

May 6, 1982

On Monday I went to the Chancery,
Serious work, dedicated work,
Work without pay.
Difficult, but comfortably done.
Done in a communal way
Working together with dedicated priests,
Working to ease the pain of God's people.
Working with God.

The next day: Tuesday
Here it is again, work for pay.
Hours of therapy, of counseling,
Commiserating with clients,
Finding, searching a path through confusion.
Shouldering anxiety, depression.
Fear and despair
Hope and faith
God's people
Working with God.

And Wednesday, no appointments, no schedule
Now the time for the great rush
The thundering horde of the undenied.
The chores, the garden, the lawns.
The cars, the repairs, the limitless.
The time for energy and strength beyond capacity.
For exhaustion and debility.
With panting followed by sickness.

Thursday is for recuperation.
A time to lick my wounds,
To wonder where the time is going,
To take stock.
This is Thursday.
Maybe something special can happen.
Something without the press of urgency,
Something creative in a choiceful sense.
God's work.

Friday. where has the week gone?
A few more appointments.
Some wrap-up counseling for the week,
Maybe the afternoon off,
Too tired to use it.
An evening for discussion, a scheduled one.
Not spontaneous, tho having spontaneity in it.
Mercifully an evening without TV.
God's people.

And Saturday.
Another wrap-up time.
For gardening and lawns and other chores.
Not a day for scheduling
For scheduling would interfere with Sunday.

And now Sunday, the day of rest.
A day for Mass, for pause and sermon.
However busy it becomes
There stays an aura about Sunday.
Of not making a drudgery of it.
Of some care for self.
No hassles should arise.
Of communing with self and others.
God's law.

INADEQUATELY PERCEIVED

May 10, 1982

I awoke this morning with the realization
That I lack foresight.
Or, that my youth was lived this way
That, especially then,
What was near
Was dear.

The perceptions, the anxieties of the moment.
The feelings, fears,
Took me - - - - and held me.
I reacted to them
And them alone
Too often.

My luck in those years was luck,
Or God or Guardian Angel.
I did look wise - - -
To others too.
My manner calm
I had integrity to some degree.

But there were so many things
To see beyond the near.
The passage of time.
The unrolling of a sequence.

And near and dear were persons -
Mother, father, brothers, - seen but not seen.
Inadequately perceived.

It was not all that bad.
It could have been worse.
But yet, so limited it was.
'Twas said by that Palermo priest
Five years ago:
The promise of baptism unrealized.

IN THE SETTING SUN

August 25, 1982

In the setting sun
As the light around me dims
As the pleasures wane
And the pains increase
When all is done - - - - - and finished
Even the important - - - - - - which all is
When the ties that bind are weak
As age and wear ever have their way
With countless wails around me
And a multitude of struggles
As strife abounds
And loss continues
There is no less
A poignant clamor
Not to be done with it
And all its proper due
But, no, a different voice
A one which seeks to cling
To hold
To keep back the inevitable
As if it were not.

A THOUGHT
(entered from an earlier time)

January 26, 1984

I accepted the opinions of others
Tho it was my life that was involved
Their sincerity was not questioned
Yet, it was my life that was involved.

ON THE DAY AFTER ANDREW'S TWENTY-EIGHTH BIRTHDAY

August 10, 1985

His mother's wont to make suggestions:
A rhyme to write, a true impression
A special time, we know is this
A momentary glimpse of Heaven's bliss.

And 'neath the surface there doth lie
A tender thought, a gentle sigh,
A memory of things past,
Of life that goes, how fast, how fast.

And deeper still, while yet atop,
A thought that will not flee or stop:
Is this the man? Is this the child?
With wrath so fierce; with mien so mild?

Aye, is it true of God's design,
That many traits are in a line,
And, for a while, must cause dismay
Till comes the blessed light of day?

If this be so, then come thou soon,
                    oh great occasion
When God's love and sure persuasion,
Truly work to make all wise
And Heaven's own goals realize.

Andy and Steve in California.

PAIN

April 6, 1986

The greatest pain I feel today
Is felt for others.
Although I have no way of knowing how someone
Feels his pain
I feel it for him.
An ache inside.
A soft, inner crying;
The body cries.
The soul.

If God must keep His distance
To give the will its reign.
If God knows all that happens,
And yet remains away.
His life must surely saddened be
To see the pain He sees.

Then prayer most meritorious must be,
That it should tell a need.
That it should give a hope,
A focus,
A goal.
And even answered be.
And, oh what joy to God,
Who is Himself set free.

VIEWPOINTS

April 10, 1986

Life has its swirling ways.
Thoughts are numerous.
Opinions abound.
Viewpoints.

The brain is capable of a thousand thoughts.
Variously held by various people.
Daily life is filled with clashing views.
So regularly as to be unnoticed.

An idea can be newly born.
And die in its first confrontation.
Another thought arrives
And carries the day.

For most
That first thought is so unrecognized
As to be subliminal
Or pre-conscious.

For most
That new creation
One's first clear view
Is allowed to slip away.

In truth, we have a battle.
A noble strife perforce.
Coming all too often
To an end which is mundane.

Must this forever be?
Must the clear, courageous slant
Be the victim
Of the trend?

Must anxiety reign ingloriously?
Statistical possibilities, probabilities?
The fear of error, king?
The lowest needs, the highest?

Must prevailing winds destroy?
Expediency proliferate?
The scuttlebutt command?
Ignorance determine?

Then should we not give thanks and glory
When within oneself
There is, that quiet recognition
Of truth beneath the tide
Or faith beneath the roar?

FOND MEMORIES

July 17, 1986

Fond memories.
One when I was seventeen
A half orphan, only recently
Away from home, a military camp - - - -
Camp Dix, New Jersey
(A place I would return to.)
A month away from home;
A large and unaccustomed break with tender ties
A prelude of things to come.
Perhaps a barrenness.
And then, from nowhere, it seemed.
Unannounced.
Unexpected, she came.
Totally unexpected!
From long miles away.
An arduous trip from Brooklyn.
A vision of tender love, of warmth,
And vulnerability, susceptibility, of wear.
And yet so young an age.
So much already suffered.
So much endured.
And so much more to come.
And whether the world is better now,
For her having been in it those years,
It surely was the better then.
So precious that it hurt.
Even now.

Does aching come with precious memory?
Or does the pain reveal itself,
At the time.
Like a premonition.
A special consciousness.
As if God pulls one aside and says,
"Here's one to remember:
Here's one you will remember."
I was maybe twelve.
Home for lunch, from P.S. 95.
(Imagine! A number to indicate all that
Precious humanity.)
It was simply beans.
With olive oil, salt and pepper.
And hard-crusted, delicious bread.
Fresh from the bakery.
My mother and I alone.
(Where were the others?)
A sense of warmth and love.
Unforgettable.
Was it merely that one time?
Or was it one of many,
With God entering in - - - -
That I would take note
And have this special Grace.

And yet again.
A soldier.
A young lieutenant
Home for a while.
Maybe prior to "shipment" overseas,
The logistics vague -   but not the enchantment.
A meal of pasta - lasagna maybe.
Delicious.
But more than that -
A felt experience -
Of tender love,
Of Grace.
An aura so intense
So overpowering -
To bring tears –
Tears to be suppressed -
To be strongly felt inside.
Why?
How?
Even now, it lies beyond my ken.

The writer and his mother probably in 1922 in New Jersey.

ON CAROL'S GRADUATION FROM NATIONAL UNIVERSITY

July 13, 1986

The war is over.
The battles won.
The striving upward
Finally done.

The goal of many months is reached.
The golden ramparts now are breached.

Is now the time for just repose
Beneath the gaze of this duck's nose?

Carol and cousin Jackie in Sicily in 1995.

A YEAR WITH EVERYTHING

July 27, 1986

The year is eighty-six.
The times are full.
A coastal whiplash does confront us
And we must bend beneath.
(I count three.)

There was a hundredth birthday.
Early on it was.
New York's Lady Liberty.
And as we watched the ships go by,
(We wondered what to do.)

A year for marking birthdays.
Grandma's eightieth at the tip,
And while the hometown is a – calling,
There's an infant on a trip.
(But the trio is a-waiting.)

And now a pyramid I see,
With weddings at each end
And on the sides are showers,
For times as yet to be.
(A triple feast is in the wings.)

The triangle's base took fifteen months to build –
Of such toil and sweat and fears
That Earth herself shook mightily
To match the Magna which was won.
(When, Oh, Lord?)

But we shall soon be leaving.
Alabama must be reached,
With Steve and Good St. Francis waiting.
(But first a party here.)

There are Mondays.
There are Tuesdays.
And there are Fridays, too.
Today, the twenty-seventh, Sunday.
(It will have to do.)

So,
Blessed be Lawrence,
Blessed by Andrew.
And Blessed be Mother too.
On your one hundred and twenty-first.
(A triple one for you.)

WE WERE LEFT IN DISARRAY

July 28, 1986

We were left in disarray,
The captain himself deserted.
Who was left to save us?
Save God, whom we saw not.

Rudderless we were,
And wandering.
And then the winds came,
Dispersing us.

A holocaust near took us.
We clung to the remnants,
And these too were scattered,
In the confusion.

And yet another was taken from us.
What was, and more could be,
The heart, the soul, the center.
The hope and inspiration.

For the strength of all
Is not in strength unlimited.
And hope a fragile thing can be,
Lest ever nourished.

A sad thing it is to see,
The wholesale floundering that overtook us then.
As Wisdom failed to send us rescue,
And we remained adrift.

Across a span of generations
Our humble trek continued.
A search for peace and love   - -
And solidarity.

And, yes, the struggle raged.
The ramparts ever stormed.
Here and there a light - -
Flickering.

There seems a time and space allotted
For these sallies forth.
Vigor too is parceled out   - -
For each adherent to the cause.

Now Wisdom counsels cease
To try to rectify the wrong.
The scar is there forever.
The wound can never heal.

It's time to cut our losses.
To take stock of what is there.
To find what there is left to us
And shelter it with care.

For while a battle rages,
And there is disarray,
The precious goes unnoticed,
And evil will hold sway.

Re-coup, re-gather and re-group then.
Tis better now than never.
And take advantage of the strength
That God holds out forever.

Embattled we have been.
And dazed we still remain.
But, God, we have your promise
That we can scotch this stain.

So, I must chart a new course.
Tomorrow, not today.
For I know not my bearings,
And fear beclouds the way.

Lord, what must be gathered?
And what must wait?
I begin to hear a message
That may show me well my fate.

Is there an unseen presence
That makes it all quite clear?
Or is it naïve hope
That registers itself here?

But, still this life abuilding,
The same message does impart,
To face each issue squarely,
Right here in my heart.

For in the heart is God discovered.
The brain is but a tool,
Which ever makes its twists and turns,
Yet can't prevent the fool.

FROM DENVER TO BIRMINGHAM
IN A 737 JET

July 30, 1986

From twenty-seven thousand feet
The distance is so great
You'd think the separation from the Earth
Could not be overcome.

Encapsulated in cocoon,
The travel mode of man today.
The insulation seems complete,
From life below.

Five miles high we are.
Closer to God.
We could be having thoughts
Removed from life's concerns.

And yet the bond remains.
I see the towns below,
And sense a kinship
With them.

There are also patterns on the ground
Which are a puzzle.
Hundreds of man-made circles.
And then no more.

For a while
The rivers wend their way
Like dendrites
From a central cell.

As I look down below
I go unnoticed by the people of these towns.
My anonymity matches
Their ignorance of me.

Understandably,
This pattern
Is explained - - - - - -
By circumstance.

And maybe habit is the reason,
For the curiosity I feel   - - -
For human life below.
As if one pressed a button
To let the juices flow.

Is it habit also, then,
Which makes me overlook that God
Is ever mindful of my welfare,
And anonymity be damned?

Or is it something more than that?
Are we programmed for this sort of thing?
To carry out His plan,
To keep to His instructions,
To love our fellow man.

ROSALIE WAS ALL NIGHT
WITHOUT THE LIGHT

August 8, 1986

Forget you.
I don't need nobody.
If you knew what I been through.
Believe me.
What I've been through.

How many times I been good to people.
Your father, God rest his soul.
How many times he help people.
Go ask your cousins.
In Sicily.

Now what?
Where am I to go?
If someone would just say,
Here, you can stay with me.
If someone would just give me a place.

What do you want me to do?
Sell my home?
For what?
For an apartment?
So, I can walk all alone in the apartment?
I love my home.
Why should I leave it?

What I been through with your father.
But I'm not going to say anything.
It's just between me.

I believe if I go to someone's home,
I should be treated special.
After all, I'm the oldest.
Cheri's mother knows how to treat a person.

And you want,   me to sell my house.
And live in an apartment.
So, I can spend a few months here!
A few months there!
I'm not a gypsy.

Believe me.
What I been through with your father.
Only God knows.

Ah, it's raining.
I go check the leaves on the drain.
Such a storm.
Last year there was such a storm on Long Island.
Rosalie was all night without the light.

I don't care.
If nobody wants to give me a party.
I give it myself.
I got the money.
See the card President Reagan sent.

1989 Stopover in New York City at JFK airport.

ON KING'S HIGHWAY
AND WEST THIRTEENTH

August 8, 1986

The kids are really restless here today.
Actually, lively more than restless
And a bit loud.
Just a bit.
Enough to have an impact.
You certainly know they're here.

All of them sub-teens, I would say.
With their mothers.
In this small branch
Of the Brooklyn Public Library.
A library with its issues and its volumes
But bureaucratically run.

There are a number of them,
The librarians.
Out where the books and people are.
And also in the back.
They are human beings all
But the library is bureaucratically run.

The children best remind us of our humanity.
The effervescence and the verve.
The librarians must perforce be tired,
Being older.
Yet, they must sometimes yearn for freedom.
But the library is bureaucratically run.

FROM ST. LOUIS TO LOS ANGELES ON A 767

August 11, 1986

As I settle into my seat on this jet airplane today,
I can see that it is time for a more jaundiced view
Of this kind of movement   - - - -
From one place to another.
And, even,
Of the purpose behind it.

Perforce,
Modern travel involves no movement - - - - -
Of the individual that is.
What moves is the box
That he sits
Or stands within.

The passenger is fed,
Or not,
Depending on the length of the trip.
Chicken or steak it used to be
Nowadays, however, due to costs,
It's apt to be a sandwich, or a salad.

The food and its serving
Is only one of many ways
That the person is helpless
To fend for himself - - - -
To make his own decisions - - - -
To deal with his own vulnerability.

There are other things
Like choosing whom to be with.
To talk to.
To be with others in friendship,
To break down the barriers,
To forego one's anonymity.

Or,
How about a walk?
I like walking.
I need the movement of it.
The meditation in it.

Walking!
Really! Fat chance!
Even if this were not a plane,
Or a car.
If it were a train, it would simply be - - -
Body movement.

No,
The mystique of modern modes of travel
Is living matter in a box - - -
Like a snake in a glass enclosure on exhibit.
Or a fish in an aquarium - - - -
Or a hamster in a rotating wheel.

The fear of flying is easily understood.
The placing of oneself in hands unknown,
On the human and technical level.
That is the great surrender,
Especially great in its obviousness - - - - -
And in the need for the suspension of anxiety.

In retrospect.
After many years of flying,
Many flights.
That alone should give pause.
Flying should be justifiable
Only after the most serious scrutiny.

This particular trip   - - - -
Requiring five flights
From Los Angeles to Denver to Birmingham
To New York to St. Louis to Los Angeles
Was made for   - - - -
Of all things   - - - -
A birthday party.
The kind of thing I might easily not have
                    crossed the street for.

Is this a valid use of human reason?
Is this the kind of thing   - - -
That God intended?
A birthday party?
A whimsical thing   - - - -
A child's thing.

I could take a walk,
In my neighborhood
Or I could garden
Or read a book
Or go to Mass
And serve God and my soul better.

I could risk my life
In more worthwhile ventures
Than to fly almost a half dozen planes,
Thirty-five thousand feet high,
And make myself this subservient
To capricious fortune.

I could better apply myself
To demanding, grueling pursuits.
Commendable and spirit-lifting
Than to suffer
This unnerving strain and drain
For some frivolity.

Although human gains are made
As friends and relatives and close family
Renew acquaintance or feast together
Or commune.
Is not the preciousness of contact of this sort
Greatly over-rated?

Do contacts of this sort, in fact, mislead?
Do contacts of this sort dissipate the true focus
Of one's goals and energies.
Do contacts of this sort
Becloud the insight
Which must be achieved?

Are contacts of this sort - - - - -
Misleading?
Denying the reality
Of the separation, which,
Without great restructuring,
Is irrevocable?

Are we not more alone
Than we would like to think we are?
And does not this aloneness
Hold promise - - -
For a greater realization - - -
Of God's presence?

Am I not, in fact,
More alone in this plane,
With two hundred strangers - - -
Than I am - - - - - walking - - - -
In my neighborhood?

How could I - - - -
Why would I - - - - -
Subject myself to not being able to walk - -
When I am not lame
To restriction, stagnation and frustration - - -
When I am free,
To idiocy when God's light is in me?

CAR SHOPPING

November 13, 1986

It's been many months.
Maybe longer.
Who knows?

I've been looking for a car to buy.
We've needed one for some time.
I failed to get one   - - -
When I should have.

I should have gotten one three or four years ago
And any time since then.
But it was easy to dissuade me.
My friend, Tonto, was against it.
After all, it was her car,
In such poor shape   - - - -
That needed replacing.
My need for a newer car
Was overlooked.

And so, again, the trials began.
Months ago.
Interrupted by our plane trip to New York,
As well as Alabama.

I've tested maybe twenty models   - - - -
Of different makes.
Some more than once
Four years ago, it was eighteen.
Altogether, thirty-five or forty different cars.

Always, there has been an obstacle.
Some apparent - - - -   some hidden.
Each one must be overcome.
But each requires time - - - -
And self-examination.

A strange business, one might say.
Yet each person must his own road travel.
I neither know, nor can attempt another way.

For a long time, it was the Japanese,
Makers of such fine cars.
But they bombed Pearl Harbor
And I could not forget - - -
Nor forgive.
Till God, to whom I turned
Wiped away my objection,
When he would no such distinction make.

Then, it was the cost,
Which to someone trained with smaller figures,
Does seem huge.
Inflation is the culprit, not the numbers.
And with an objective spirit - - -
Looking at every sum,
In truth, there is, as well, an increase
In the means.

And just two days ago, discovered,
Was yet another block.
How could I face the possibility,
That having purchased a modern-day chariot,
I would then regret
Some great mistake
In it.

This time I called for help.
It came noiselessly.
My daughter calmly pointed out,
What I already know,
That only matters of great moment
Deserve such concern.
And, yesterday, my brother noted,
That mistakes can be undone.

I could have managed from here on out, I think,
If something had not struck me yet again,
An hour or so ago.
A sadness lies beneath it   - - - - -
Possibly sinister.
I do not know.
It is all too soon to tell.

I do not know its form.
Perhaps a memory of times past.
Perhaps a deeply-imbedded facet of my life.

The thought   - - or was it a preconscious aura - -
Of uncollected things   - - -
Of things left over   - - - -
Someone having died.

And then, I saw my parents   - - -
Separately.
First, the one, then the other   - - -
As ideas, perhaps.

My father having died,
He left his things behind.
His coat, which then I wore.
His shoes, books, and all.
The circumstances of his death
Made for an emotional clutter.
A clutter which attached itself to things - - -
Like the coat I wore to college - - - -
The next year.
An overcoat whose weight was more - - - -
Than merely physical.

And suddenly, I saw again that scene,
Wherein I had presented my mother, in hospital,
With a special gift, a red cashmere cardigan - - -
And her reluctance to put it on.
Painfully unspoken it was:
The fear that she would not live to wear it.
And I, impatient with that unspoken thought.
I may have prevailed.
I cared not, then, for any clutter,
Left upon her death.
A death, the thought of which,
Had not yet reached consciousness.

And so we may have come full circle.
The onion peels once more - - - -
Revealing, and perhaps redeeming in one motion
As it lays the burden bare.

BLIND

January 27 - February 23, 1987

A year ago, this month
While sitting at table
An occurrence of striking import
To me, as an individual, at least potentially,
And to my family and friends.

I went blind,
In one eye,
The left,
For a minute.

Nothing new.
It had happened to me before.
Maybe a few times a year
Maybe for a few years.

But, bringing it up was new.
And that particular newness
Was to have consequences,
Some apparent   - - -
And others still unfolding

Beyond the general startlement
There lay another thought.
Also new.
That I should seek to know
Something about it.
This would involve others.

In retrospect, it seems fair to say,
That those four of us at table that night
Could see that the truly significant others
Would be the physicians - - - -
The eye specialists.

Within a week
I had presented myself to one - - - -
And undergone tests - - - - -
And been apprised of dangers:
Permanent blindness.

Another week, another specialist.
More tests, more warnings - - - - - -
But referral now, to higher authority,
The internal specialist.
My very own.

More tests - - - - - more warnings
Besides referral for more tests,
A decision that I would medicate - - - -
Myself - -
With serious drug,
Whose awesome power
Stunned me
To refuse.

The tests and warnings continued
And in the midst of these came
Yet another episode or two
Of blindness.
Months passed.

The atmosphere was ever ominous.
The tests ever painful.
One physician, a neurologist,
Made timid agreement with my refusals.
But, would I medicate with aspirin?
Daily?
He wrote my continued refusal down,
For the record.

I have experienced many crises.
And more than my share of tragedies.
Or, so it seems.

A consensus develops
In a crisis
If one is blessed with others
Who try to help
And still others
Who very much care.
Who love.

The consensus is an all-out support
For the welfare, the well-being
Of the loved one.
But courage is involved
And while some matters
Are accommodated more easily
By the courageous acts of others
This is not true of all.

On occasion, there will arise a crisis
Which must be faced alone.
And courage is required,
And often, there is none.

Not that courage is allotted
To just a favored few,
But simply that, quite often
It is hidden from one's view.
Not merely cowardice,
But confusion interferes,
With skeletons unknown,
Whose very anonymity disturbs us.

Human progress is slow.
Yet, a small change can yield large results.
To move an inch can yield a mile.
To move an inch can be the moving of a mountain,
Psychologically,
Or spiritually.
But,
It takes time.

In man's primeval past,
There was emptiness in the vastness.
There was emptiness in the stillness,
In the simplicity,
In the isolation.

And, later, came the gathering.
And communities formed.
And life was richer.

Life in a community requires
Social patterns of behavior - - - - -
Systems to enfold the richness
And leaders to implement,
To guide
And serve.

Over the millennia
And the centuries,
It was never easy.
The task has been too great for us.
For leaders, guides and servers.
For all of us.
We do quite well considering.
We need much better, though.

As we advance, we falter.
The progress cannot be seen by all.
Although it depends upon the light.
Which facet do we see?
And, how is it, overall?

Were it not for the Holy Spirit
We'd get nowhere.
Were it not for our free will
We'd be slaves.

Leaders and led alike are human.
The needs are alike for both - - -
Courage, humility, knowledge.

The desire for security is understandable,
The need for expediency as well.
And fear is human,
And practical.
But fear and expediency cannot reign,
Nor the grasp for security override all.
Humility must be close at hand - - - -
And surrender.

Today, the spectre of blindness,
The fear and terror of it,
Has receded.
The agony of decision has passed.
The surrender justified,
Now.
The exercise of courage will be forgotten.
No matter.
Past memories of great acts
May well be worthless for the future.
The future needs its own mix,
Its blend of virtues.
And spontaneity.
The Holy Spirit, never resting,
Does not exist in frozen form.
And courage needs, to some extent,
Be rated,
Like the makers of a movie,
Or an opera, or symphony,
Or like a baseball team:
What have you done for me, lately?

I CINISARI

March, 1987

Once in a while
I think back
To times before my time
To the seven or so children
That my great grandmother bore.

At least six of them were sons
Perhaps, there was a daughter
And from these offspring
There issued
The migrating generation.

My grandfather's name was Joseph.
Pippinu in Sicilian.
Him I never saw.
I'm told he came across the sea
And found this country wanting.

Back, then, to the homeland.
He took his family with him,
And their return, upon his death, soon after,
Further diminished the clan's presence
In the ancestral town.

Others had come before,
Their children marrying and begetting
They set their roots here
Wistfully remembering
That Cinisi had been home to them,
For a dozen generations.

Centuries had passed
Since the clan had settled there
And I'd hear tell
Of oranges and lemons
Of special size and flavor,
Of Zi Coco's great house,
Of the long walk,
Over mountains,
From Cinisi to Palermo.

Their youth was spent there - - - - -
My father's generation
Their hearts, their souls
Were somehow trapped there - - -
Never free, never available to them here - - -
Not quite intact.

What they had going for them in New York
And thereabouts,
As they settled in,
Was what they could bring with them:
Their relationships
And their patterns of behavior,
Their perceptual habits
Their memories.

Had they not had each other
Difficult lives would have been worse,
Perhaps.
Unless they could have made the transition
As, later, their children did.

Of my father's generation
All but one or two settled in this country.
Almost all were males.
I knew of only one or two females.
All were married to Italians,
Though Zi Rusina was born here.
Almost all married Sicilians.
My mother was the rare Neapolitan.

And so, we spoke four languages
In our home.
My father spoke Sicilian to my mother.
My mother spoke Neapolitan back to him,
And to us.
The formal language was Italian (with guests)
And we children spoke English to our parents,
Sicilian to our relatives,
And absorbed the others
To some extent.

There must have been, at least - - - - -
Twenty first cousins,
In my father's generation.
Of course, they knew each other,
And one or two would come - - - -
All the way from Sicily,
On an occasional visit.
In those days
The twenties and the thirties - - - -
There was little or no traveling back,
On the part of those
Who lived here.
Surprising.

They talked, they walked,
They socialized.
Ate some meals together
Spent part of the holidays together.
I remember poker games and others
During the Christmas holidays.
And sometimes of a Christmas
Or New Year's Eve
There'd be a midnight vigil
Followed by freshly cooked
Sausages and dough puffs
With powdered sugar.

Church-going was not as prominent then
As later it became.
My father, in the years I best remember,
Was anti-clerical.
Yet, somehow, the Church was there.
Basic - - - even prominent.
Religious events, like Communion,
Were special celebrations.
I remember my older brother's Confirmation.
My parents threw a big party.
I remember the special foods.
One was suffritto.

The weeks and months I spent
Preparing for my First Communion - - -
I was almost eleven - - -
Was a holy time for me.
I remember and feel it well,
To this day.
I feel the warmth of it,
And the faith.
And the specialness.

When my father died - - - - - -
Despairingly,
Tragically,
And left behind
A family stunned,
And saddened,
And I, not yet seventeen
And negligent in the practice
Of my faith,
Reached within - - - -
I found it there,
Still.

From time to time,
The clan spread out
Across this land.
Chicago first
The Jersey Marinellos went.
And, later,
After the Great War
Two of us
To California.
And now, even Florida.

There are hundreds of us now,
But scattered.
There are hundreds of us now,
But the bonds of common experience,
Common dinners
Parties - - - - -
Baseball games
Stickball games, and handball
Is gone.
Except in the elders.
In memory.

Brothers give way to first cousins
And first cousins to second
And to third
And fourth.
Recognition fades
And, perforce, the bonds weaken.
There is no turning back the tide.

There is a sadness in this
A sadness somehow justified
Not merely in its own contemplation
But in the gladness
Which is felt
On those rare occasions
Of reunion
Which re-create the aura
Of what was good
In days gone by.

The fact remains, nevertheless,
That each life has its own destiny
Each new family its own path
Its own experiences.
That each person,
Each family,
By its very nature
Grows.
And in growing - - - - -   - - - - - spreads,
And leaves for its own horizons.

In this continuing,
And increasingly-mobile world,
Some there are who stay behind
And live their particular brand of life.
I wonder what it's like for them.
Or, do we all,
Or, most of us,
Eventually,
Come to that point
And rest?

MRS. CLEMENTE

March 18, 1987

Today, the eighteenth of March
A special day, being, as it is, situated
Between the Saint's days
Of Patrick and Joseph,
I heard played, on the radio,
A recording of Debussy's
"Pavane pour une enfante defunte"
The conductor was Giulini,
The orchestra, the London Philharmonia.
Only the other day
My daughter had said,
She'd heard that Giulini's wife
Had died.

And now this recording
Of so tender a piece,
Made, the announcer said,
Just this past year
Kindles the imagination
And makes one think
How this devoted couple
Experiences, poignantly now,
A reciprocating and recurring homage
Each to the other
And evokes the memory, as well,
Of a moment, over fifty years ago,
When, as a child,
I heard Mrs. Clemente say,
On the news of her brother's death,
"Murriu com un aceddu"
The very essence of Giulini's phrasing
Of this now more tender work.

THE TRIP

May 5-8, 1987

We just got back yesterday
From a trip
A nine-day long trip
To Bridgeport,
To Grass Valley
To Carmel, Cambria, and Solvang.

The usual.
We needed to get away.
We've needed to get away for months.
This time we made it.

Also, we took Jessica and Joel.
Returning them home to Bridgeport.
Bridgeport, a lot more pleasant,
Being less arctic-like in temperature,
Than it was in winter last year,
When the temperature went below
Zero.

As I think on it,
Day by day,
It seems that this trip was momentous,
In many ways.
Maybe all trips are momentous
And yet pass without notice
Unless one is in a bard-like frame of mind
Like I've been of late.

To start with,
Aside from the wear and tear
That driving, even an Alfa,
Entails for me,
And also the ticket for speeding,
Perhaps my first, at age sixty-six,
Which I received in Lancaster
Probably related to the Alfa - - - - -
A really fast car,
There was the fact that,
On our first evening in Bridgeport
Andy was fired - - - or let go,
From his quite recently-acquired job
As a seller of fish bait and things
Which he had, as yet,
Not tried his hand at.

His boss had simply called
That Sunday night, April twenty-sixth,
And informed him that they had come
To the parting of the ways.

Now,
That had some dramatic impact.
Besides the sadness and dejection there was shock.
And yet, I found what followed
Even more impressive - - - - more telling.

Within moments,
Andy decided to call someone else
Who might supply him
With an immediate replacement job
As a gardener.

I am grateful that, somehow,
He accepted my counsel not to call.
A counsel based on the intuition that,
A person should be able to remain jobless,
For at least a little while.
Being fired or laid off is not that uncommon.

Besides,
He was sick,
Had been for four or five days
Which is what led
To his not being at work
And, hence, being let go.
And, being sick, I thought,
He would have found it difficult
To manage a hard day's work,
The very next day.

In fact, the very next day, indeed,
We went fishing.
He, Joel, Mom and I.
And out of three fishermen (Mom was watching)
Andy was the only one
To catch a fish.
A moderately small trout
We had that night, for dinner.

Before dinner, however,
We, all of us, made a trek to Walker,
A town that has a few ranches
And farms
And saw Lori's horse
And met the people there.

On the way back, with a new perspective,
There seemed to be many more ranches,
Farms and settlements than one would see
Coming from a crowded metropolis
Such as L.A.

And, the next day, we made our way,
Over the mountain passes.
Snow was all around.
And into the Gold country,
The Mother Lode.
To Placerville and Auburn
To Coloma where gold was found, in 1848,
And Grass Valley, where we stayed the night.

It was in Grass Valley that I realized
That further travel in those mountains,
Along those mountain roads,
Was too strenuous for me to spend more time on it.
And so we left the next day,
Leaving that corner with the motel
And shopping centers
And restaurants
All isolated from the town itself
A not uncommon thing
As one travels by car these days.

From Grass Valley we went to Marysville
And Yuba City and Davis with its university.
We took a route recommended, probably,
By a truck driver,
By way of the Best Western motels,
And on quiet roads
Saw places I had been curious about
For many years.
All viable little communities.

And so we came to Monterey.
Picturesque and historic and alive.
And Carmel, a precious town,
With its cool clear air,
Its active shops and galleries
Teeming with motels and restaurants
Its sweetly-dramatic beach
With its grand sweep
To rival Monterey's.

But it would be hard to find,
Even in Palermo,
The view that meets the eye when,
Driving north from Carmel, on Route One
You are confronted by that immense arc,
That broad expanse - - - - - - - -
Of Monterey Bay.
There for the asking - - - -
A gift.
Unexpected.

Monterey has its history,
With its Fisherman's Wharf,
Which is not so much for fishermen, these days,
As it is for restaurants and tourists.

We had dinner at the Wharfside restaurant
And talked with Nino Palma,
Part owner,
Who knew the one-time police chief,
Frank Marinello, possibly a distant relative,
And we visited
The brand-new Monterey Aquarium.

Carmel has its mission.
A solid religious anchor it is,
With Father Serra buried there.
But also, Carmel has taste.
Exquisite.
Both in shops and restaurants
Built round its proprietors
And their clientele
And a community spirit.
An appealing spot, along with Monterey
And the Carmel Valley
For us, who wish to re-settle.
Even so - - - - - it is difficult to leave
Our home and roots of thirty years.

Another favorite spot for us,
Cambria.
We arrived there next in a windstorm
That seemed capable of tearing the car door
Off its hinges.

Deliciously cool
Cambria offered its own surprises.
That first night's windstorm knocked down power
lines
And left us without light or power for two hours.

The next morning
On a leisurely walk
Near the beach
We checked out motels for the future
And stopped at an art gallery
Whose artist proprietor was
Arthur Van Rhyn
A former Northridge engineer who came North
To follow his calling as an artist.

After a while
A poet mystic friend came by,
Aged 70, Derek Wordsworth-Topham,
Who told us he had lived
A number of other lives
Going as far back as
Three to four thousand years.
That he'd once been
A Roman legionnaire
And that, in this life,
He had come into the presence
Of Christ.

We discussed history
And he indicated that, yes,
King Arthur had indeed existed
That Greeks had early come to Britain
And Cambria was the Roman name
For the last Celtic kingdom.

We talked of restaurants and dinner.
The mystic recommended Moustache Pete
In town,
But the artist insisted that
In the quasi ghost town of Harmony
The Pasta Factory was the place to go.

That afternoon we had a fine lunch
At the Moonstone Gardens Inn
And after a laundry visit
(Which included a talk with Dean,
Another seventy year old,
Jack of all trades, including
Amateur actor)
And a nap,

We found our way to
This apparently deserted town,
This Harmony
And found located in a non-descript building
An excellent Italian restaurant.
Talked with the lovely New Zealand waitress,
Later, with the proprietress
And witnessed a man feeding his wife
Who was helpless in a wheelchair.

This trip had a grinding quality to it.
I think all trips do.
We must keep going
We must keep to some sort of schedule,
Yet another stretch of driving,
Another motel
And the desire, increasing,
Now that we've been gone awhile,
To return home.
Our home.
So comfortable in its familiarity.
The traveller's ultimate goal.

There was only Solvang left.
We arrived on Sunday
After Mass and a Knights of Columbus breakfast
At Cambria's Santa Rosa Church.
Talked with Father Sweeney,
An ancient fellow, and very tall.
Met Art and Mary Pearson
Who offered their home to us
For future visits.
There was a super malt in Pismo Beach.

That evening we walked the quiet streets
Of Solvang.
The tourists gone.
A three week old Italian restaurant,
Massimi,
Is where we had a light dinner
And talked at length with the hostess wife.
Her husband was Massimiliano Muller
Whose grandfather was German.

Next morning, we visited the Mission,
Santa Ynez.
Bought yet another two aebleskiver pans
And were given a tour
By a capable real estate saleswoman,
Karen Voorhis,
Expecting in August.
Then lunch and the trip home
And soon begins again
The back and forth
The pros and cons
Of relocating.

COMPACT DISCS

May 15, 1987

One of the ways you know,
Nowadays,
That you've become antiquated,
Is that, yet again,
You must update yourself.

Yesterday,
My wife of some forty years informed me
That most record companies
Were no longer making L.P.s
Only discs.

Being, as they say, a music lover,
All my life,
I've been pushed around
By the jabs of change
More than once.

And yet,
I was in the very vanguard of music listening
When, over thirty-five years ago,
Along with my friend, Stan Magagnosc,
I set up one of the first high fidelity systems.

The next time around, however,
The impetus for change came from without.
And so I switched to that something new.
Stereophonic high fidelity.
But, reluctantly.

Quadrophonics I have successfully avoided.
But, the disc played by laser beam
Is another story.
There are some things you can avoid
And some you can't.

That is, if I want to keep abreast
Of the new recordings.
If I want to continue listening to music.
Which I don't do too much nowadays, anyway.
Except to attend live concerts.

And so there are choices one is free to make,
Even in those more crucial and more subtle areas,
Like personality and also, relationships.
One is often free to change his ways,
Or remain the same.

To remain the same in some facet of one's make-up
Often has merit.
Especially when to change to the newer mode
Means a form of idiocy,
Or, even, disaster.

The older ways look pretty good, these days.
The newer ways,
Ever on the cutting edge
Ever on the windows of innovation,
Are often adopted without careful thought.

Yes, the newer ways have their pitfalls.
Today's world is littered with their debris.
Lives shattered.
Lives lost.
The eagerness not to miss out backfires.

The eagerness to relate to others
Needs to be tempered.
Tempered by a need to relate to self.
And, more important still - - - - -
To God.

But this applies, as well,
To that refusal to give up
Those quirks that each of us possesses.
Those quirks that serve only poorly
Our sometimes-mistaken selves.

Most of us can be charming
Affable and reasonable.
We can be courteous to strangers
And compassionate with our friends.
We can be bosom buddies.

Present company excepted,
I know some people
Whose quirks and habits,
Weird and intolerable though they may be
Are known only to that unfortunate few
To whom they are close - - - - -
By birth, work, marriage,
Or by being neighbors.
The world beyond suspects nothing.

There is a poignant irony in all this
For those very traits,
Which such disservice give to him who has them,
Are jealously guarded against all entreaties.

The years go by and they remain in citadel.
The protests and admonitions fail and fade away.
The worst that could occur
          becomes more imminent.
The hapless traits are near to permanency.

There is, apparently, a limit to the effort
That family and sometimes even friends can make.
They finally either fade away or bend,
For their resolve was anything but unlimited.

Ah, yes.
The last act can be ironic.
We age.
And, as we age, we clutch so desperately,
So fervently to our bosoms
Those treacherous quirks
Those attitudes
Those would-be precious symbols
Of our integrity,
Of unreasoning fear and pride
Like Cleopatra's asp.

(May 18, 1987
Pope John Paul II's
67th birthday)

RING-A-LEVIO

May 23, 1987

Sixty-seven years old today.
I was there when Italo Balbo
Came with his fleet of planes, in 1933,
And landed at Floyd Bennet Field.

That same year, Primo Carnera,
A heavyweight boxer
Wrested the title
From Jack Sharkey.

In 1927, next to my brother's hospital bed,
On crystal radio earphones,
I heard the sounds of the crowd in Paris,
When Charles Lindberg landed there.

That same year
I heard the Tunney-Dempsey fight
On one of the first cabinet radios
In Zi Minicu's house on Ninth Street.

Earlier, in Lyndhurst,
I remember being at the opening
Of a movie theatre.
A major social event in those days.

We moved to Brooklyn in the late twenties.
There was the Hoover-Smith presidential race.
Hoover won.
Was my father a Republican then?

From Sixth Street we moved to Seventh.
(Our cousins, or a few of them,
Were clustered in four houses on Ninth Street.)
Next came Fifth Street and Avenue U.

We had ice boxes, not refrigerators.
The iceman came with a block of ice
Every day or two.
And we emptied the water pan below.

This meant no ice cream
As we know it today.
Ice cream was available once or twice a year
From passing street vendors.

Autos were rarely to be seen in those days.
The horse and wagon was the delivery mode.
Besides ice for ice boxes
They helped deliver milk and hawk vegetables.

Wakes were held in the homes of the deceased.
Funerals were dignified walking affairs,
Accompanied by a marching band
Of fifteen or twenty musicians.

We played a lot of handball in the summer -
And softball and stickball,
Caddy, box ball, touch football.
Ring-a-levio in the evenings.

And now, those days are gone.
No one seems to repeat
What once we did
Or were.

Newer generations, newer modes.
Religions we'd only read about before.
Asiatics, colonials, Hispanics.
The south of the border peoples.

These are the years of great migrations.
War has been the great dislocator.
Large populations have meant large migrations.
People pushed and bruised - - - - - - - - escaping.

These have been the mobile years, too
Of a mobile people.
By car, train, and plane
We transplant ourselves - - - - - - - - more and more.

America - - - - ever-changing - - - - - ever renewing.
America - - - ever immigrant - - - ever replenished.
The America of many faces - - - - -
Many tongues.

If the next sixty-seven years
Bring as much change
As the last
Who will recognize the land of my youth?

THE TRIP TO ALABAMA IN 1987

June 16, 1987

We've been to Alabama twice before.
The first time we came
By way of New York and Atlanta.
The next time was by way of Denver.
This time we came via Nashville
On American Airlines.

The purpose was to visit Steve
Because purpose there was for this trip.
But to say we came to visit
Doesn't tell it all.
Putting it that way would be a good example
Of saying something
While saying nothing.

We came for many reasons
Steve had been urging us to come.
His mother felt he was homesick.
Also, that we should be better informed
On his plans to propose,
In getting to know Ann's family,
In getting a feel for things.

We certainly got that feel for things.
In Alabama, people speak Alabamese.
The ones we met held some sort of
Religious convictions,
Strongly,
Or, clingingly.

It seemed customary to have conversation
Centered on their church
On the people there
On all sorts of details
And happenings
A practice, which,
Were one to witness it in a Catholic,
Would seem odd.

Also, religious conviction may have extended
To wine - - - - - - -
Which meant meals without it.
And though the meals were sumptuous - - - - -
They were difficult.
It makes one wonder if oil and water
Will ever mix.

The Scotts are fine people
As are Grady and Jane Friday
Bill and Margaret Smith.
We were also treated to a very fine lunch
At the one-time governor's mansion
On the university campus
By Attlee and Betty Jefcoat.

There were a number of striking facets
To this trip to Tuscaloosa.
There was the visit to Tannehill
A civil war historical site
Where I learned more clearly how iron is made
And where we read that an Italian colony
Had years back settled in Ensley,
Now a section of Birmingham.

There was the murder of Chanda Fehler
A friend of Ann's
Drowned in the river.
There was the Scotts' home,
Amidst a forest,
And their mountain cabin, on a river.

Mass at St. Francis, on Sunday, was exciting.
Father Angelo, a Salesian, was visiting
From Guatemala.
Father Kevin had some of us say
From whence we were visiting
And he had the children join him
At the altar.

The plane trip ended with an on-screen depiction
Of the last few minutes of the plane's landing
The landing gear, the pilot said, seemed in trouble
And the back and forth exchanges
Between pilot and control tower
On the heavy load of fuel
And the need, perhaps, for emergency measures
Was unsettling to those who were aware of it.
I had to face the prospect of death
In a few minutes,
And was able to accept it.
I am grateful.

We used the Flyaway
And the old and trusted
Red Fiat 124
And were soon home.

And now, there is a lingering thought
Gleaned from impressions, conversations - - -
From my own perusals - - - - -
Of present and of past.
The understandable shock at rape and murder.
The tales of attacks attempted and avoided,
Though some were not.
The understandable concern
The understandable arming of women
With hand guns.
The southern courtesy towards women.
The general courtesy towards one another
Given and expected in return.
The tradition of chivalry
From early beginnings.
Memories from my days in the military
Times of impulsiveness and challenges
And rage.

Is violence to be viewed, then,
As one aspect of gallantry?
Does noble loyalty sometimes lead to war?
Was slavery not the issue, then   - - - -
Nor even independence,
After all?

Steve in San Diego.

TODAY'S WORLD

June 30, 1987

There is a risk in any discipline
In any system of thought
In the development of a habit
Or habitual mode
Like the telling of lies
Or becoming trained
To be a physician - - - -
To be a teacher, in today's world.

Especially in today's world
Where to become a caterer
Or a clerk.
An auto mechanic
Or even a philosopher,
Writer or composer
Union organizer, manufacturer, politician
May, and often does mean,
To be that thing, that role
And not oneself.

The demand for efficiency is behind it
And the need for predictability.
Also, loyalty to a cause.
Or to an agency
Or person.
Especially efficiency
Because efficiency presumes productivity
And productivity - - - profitability.
For someone, or everyone - - - - -
Or nearly everyone.

The need for security in a materialistic world
Is met by material things.
The need to belong in an alien world
Is achieved by becoming an alien.
The need to be protected from insecurity,
Indigence, anxiety, and the like
Requires the making of a protective shield
And to become that shield - - - -
Oneself.

In all this
We shed our humanity
Or lose it
Or keep it covered, stifled.
Even hidden.

TOO MANY THINGS

July 7, 1987

Too many things to do
My life in modern-day California
        involves me in too many things.
This is shown by my feeling harassed,
            by my feeling tired,
By my failure to give adequate thought
        and time to those important things
            that require it and that involve
                more subtle dimensions
By my failure to do those things that I want to do
        like writing poetry
            and spending time in New York
By my failure to avoid those things of little merit
        like mowing lawns and edging them,
            by going through newspapers,
                in an effort, partially,
                    to move them further on,
                        like an assembly line.

I wonder, I wonder
        is all this a necessary price I must pay
            for the benefits I otherwise derive from
                owning my own home,
                    like a degree of privacy.
And, also, the benefit of some degree
            of physical and mental health
                to be derived from chores
                    of various kinds?

ARANCI

July 13 - August 12, 1987

Funerals today.
A far cry from yesteryear
When tears and lamentations
Were the rule,
When shock and disbelief
And a sense of misery and loss
Engulfed the bereaved.
When the food that solicitous friends
Would bring
Went untouched.
Such was the grief.

Relatives came and stayed.
Every night was a vigil.
All through the night
The suffering - - -
The relative quiet
Here and there a word
In muffled tones
Usually about the deceased
As Zi Ninu said of Zi Turiddu
"Me frati ci piacivunu l'aranci
E unu c'infradiciu."

Without the newly deceased
The future looked grim
And often was.
Life went on
But it was a life with a cloud
Hanging over it.
Readjustment took years - - - - -
As did mourning, with its symbols
Black dresses, black ties, black armbands - - -
Black everything.

The air hung heavy
With an emotional weight
Which could be felt physically
A psychological impact
Even spiritual
A burden on the soul
And yet, given the burden,
The soul could lift itself - - -
Could shoulder what was given.
In faith.

Just recently,
We attended two funerals
On consecutive days.
The first was for Russell Mangia
Dead of a heart attack at fifty-eight
Leaving behind wife, children
Brothers, sister, friends, acquaintances.
And then, there was Mary Dring, aged seventy - - -
Death due to multiple ills.
Left behind were husband, children
And many grandchildren
As well as friends and acquaintances.

In each instance, the air was not as heavy
The mourners sad instead of somber
The focus of concern may have been on
Those closest to the deceased - - - -
Whose absence would now be daily felt.
But there were other stirrings too - - - -
Positive ones - - - upbeat
Faith was there
Faith in the future
Faith in another life
A life with way stations
Where others go before.

These days, in Catholic America
There seems to be an overt awareness
That what binds us together - - - -
Besides the ties of family - - - -
The ties of clan - - - -
Is a communal tie
The glue of a community of faith.
And beyond this tie
Are the connections to all the others - - - -
The Jews, the Protestants, the atheists.
All come together - - - - to lend support
And, somehow, to prevail.

In the past few decades
There has been a striking change
A curious change, yet welcome.
Instead of an over-riding concern for the bereaved-
And their being able to partake of nourishment
There is a communal meal
For everyone who cares to come
After the funeral Mass, after the actual burial,
Usually at the home of the deceased
Or a close relative.

The change has been salutary
There is a chance to talk - - to compare notes.
The deceased has been laid to rest.
A kind of relief is felt - - - -
Which is communicated and intuitively broadcast,
Among those gathered.
In fact, the mourners are transformed.
They now become more - - - -
People who have come together for a limited time
Who must touch base again
Before they part.

I wonder, too, if this luncheoning together
Is responsible for a change that has occurred
In those hours which come before it - - - -
These past few years,
In what surrounds the church service
For, intermixed with the Mass
Between the readings and after - - - - -
There has developed a kind of testimonial
Given by people who are present,
That is, some of them.
Anecdotal, touching, emotional
And sometimes humorous.
But somehow, so uplifting, so inspiring.
Curious it is that we remain in this silence,
And yet, receive so many messages.

August 12, 1987

The writer probably on the campus of Claremont
Graduate School in the early 1950's.

PREVIOUS BOOKS BY THE AUTHOR

Unlike the Vikings

Casta Diva

GrandMa and the Miracles

The Bird and the Squirrel

RIVERSHORE BOOKS

Website:
www.rivershorebooks.com

Blog:
blog.rivershorebooks.com

Facebook:
www.facebook.com/rivershore.books

Twitter:
www.twitter.com/rivershorebooks

Email:
Jansina@rivershorebooks.com

---

www.ingramcontent.com/pod-product-compliance
Lightning Source LLC
Chambersburg PA
CBHW060944040426
42445CB00011B/1001